Beauty and the Beast

AF584081

George Ivanoff

Illustrated by Diane Le Feyer

Once upon a time, there was a story about a beautiful girl and a beast.
It was called 'Beauty and the Beast'.

Sarah and Joe went to the library
to read the story.
As they started to read ...

...a fairy appeared!
"I am Fifi the Fairytale Fixit Fairy," she said.
"Something is wrong with this story.
Can you help me fix it?"

Fifi waved her wand.
Sarah and Joe fell through the pages of the book and into the story.

They landed outside a castle.
A mean looking beast burst through the door and ran towards them.

Sarah and Joe were scared.
Fifi looked worried, too.

The beast opened its jaws wide, as if to roar... but nothing came out.

“What’s wrong?” asked Sarah.
“Sore throat,” the beast whispered.

"Oh no," said Joe.
"A beast that can't roar isn't very scary."
"We need to fix this problem
before Beauty arrives," said Fifi.

“Lemon tea with honey,” said Sarah.
“That’s what my mum drinks
when she’s got a sore throat.”

The beast shook his head.
“Lemons,” he whispered. “Yuck!”

"Fairy dust," said Fifi.
"Mix it with some water and gargle.
It always works for me."
"No!" whispered the Beast.
"Dust makes me sneeze."

"What about this?" asked Joe,
pulling a throat lolly out of his pocket.
"I had a sore throat last week and
I've got one lolly left over."

The beast sucked on the lolly and smiled.
Then he opened his mouth wide and roared.

“Thank you for fixing the story,” said Fifi.
“Now let’s go home.”
“Quickly!” said Joe.
“That beast has really bad breath!”